DAY OF THE Flymo

by Paddy Campbell

Day of the Flymo was first performed at Live Theatre,
Newcastle on Wednesday 8 April 2015.

SAMUELFRENCH-LONDON.CO.UK
SAMUELFRENCH.COM

About the Original Production

What do you do when the state decides it's going to take over from your Mam?

Day of the Flymo was first performed at Live Theatre from Wednesday 8 to Saturday 11 April, 2015. The cast included talented young actors from Live's Youth Theatre supported by a professional cast including a former Youth Theatre member:

LIAM: Kalem Patterson is 13 and from Ryton. He has been attending Live's Youth Theatre for one year and also attends Stage School.

BECCA: Tezney Mulroy is 17 and from Newcastle. She has been in Live's Youth Theatre for two years and is studying a Level 3 Degree in Acting at college.

CLARA: Sophie Pitches is 16 and from North Shields. She has been in Live's Youth Theatre for three years and is studying A-level Drama at sixth form.

KAREN: Jill Dellow is a former member of Live's Youth Theatre and is now a professional actress. Jill's work at Live Theatre includes *Chalet Lines, Write Stuff* and *Tyneside Stories*.

BEN: Akemnji Ndifornyen is a professional actor who has worked with the National Theatre, Southwark Playhouse and the BBC.

Writer Paddy Campbell
Director Paul James
Assistant Director Rachel Glover
Designer Phil Green
Lighting Designer Drummond Orr
Sound Designer Dave Flynn
Production Manager Drummond Orr
Creative Producer Graeme Thompson
Stage Manager Adam Johnston
Deputy Stage Manager Heather Robertson
Technical Manager Dave Flynn
Technician Sam Stewart
Technical Apprentices Craig Spence & Tristan Gaines
Costume Supervisor Lou Duffy
Professional Casting Lucy Jenkins CDG & Sooki McShane CDG

A word from the writer

Some years ago I spoke with Paul James, Live Theatre's Associate Director of Education & Participation, about writing a play looking at the lives of young people in the care system. I was particularly interested in writing about the point at which a young person is placed in the care of their local authority. I worked as a Residential Child Care Officer in a children's home in Newcastle for eight years. Before a child was placed in the home, their social worker would send us referral documents, which would give a potted history of their lives. This was done under headings such as health, education and identity, with a description of the circumstances leading up to their placement. By necessity the language used tended to be bland reportage, its utilitarianism blunting the edges of the lives they described. I must have read hundreds of these reports during my time there. It was a single line from one of them which gave me the opening scene to this play and it grew from there. With *Day of the Flymo*, I really wanted to highlight the gulf that can exist between the report and the person.

I've been asked if I've gone about things any differently in writing for actors that are part of Live's Youth Theatre and the honest answer is not at all. I hope I've written characters that would provide a challenge for any actor. We've recently started initial rehearsals with Tezney, Kalem and Sophie. Their commitment and bravery in tackling these parts has been truly outstanding and I feel confident Paul and Rachel will continue to draw increasingly brilliant performances from them. I am very excited for Jill and Akemnji to join us and for full rehearsals to begin.

I would also like to thank Max Roberts and Gez Casey who have greatly helped the development of this play.

Paddy Campbell

A word from the director

When Paddy Campbell approached me with the idea of writing a play about young people in care I was naturally excited by the prospect, especially with the huge success of *Wet House* at Live Theatre and on tour. Paddy's writing is hard-hitting, smacks of authenticity and unpalatable truths. His ability to constantly shift from pathos to dark humour is a gift which any director would relish. Like *Wet House*, *Day Of The Flymo* gives audiences an insider view of an environment that Paddy knows about and has worked in. The piece poses some big questions about young people caught up in the care system.

Paddy has had a long association with Live Theatre, which goes back to 2007 when he completed Live Theatre's *Introduction to Playwriting* course. He has worked extensively with the company ever since, particularly with the Education & Participation team where he has written short pieces for the Youth Theatre and has supported young writers to develop plays through our flagship writing programmes for young people. Paddy has had an amazing journey and it's been great witnessing his growth into a major new talent.

Day of the Flymo started life as a selection of scenes for a 30 minute script-in-hand performance in March 2014 to test the material in front of a young audience. The piece was performed by members of Live's Youth Theatre supported by a professional cast. The audience were gripped by the performance and the post show discussion assured us that we had something special on our hands, which would challenge young actors and engage a diverse audience. Following this Paddy was commissioned to develop the piece into a full length play. I think *Day of the Flymo* is a real gem; a compelling drama with great characters and some fantastic scenes. What else could a director and actors ask for?

I hope you enjoy reading the play text of *Day of the Flymo* but plays are written to be performed and I look forward to seeing and hearing about many other productions in the future.

Paul James
Director of *Day of the Flymo*
Associate Director of Education & Participation, Live Theatre

See page 90 onwards for group discussion points and character exercises linked to the play.

About Live Theatre

Live Theatre is recognised as one of the great new writing producing theatres on the international stage and is deeply rooted in Newcastle/Gateshead where we are based.

We believe that creativity and cultural engagement are central to the lives of individuals and arts and culture should be recognised, supported and celebrated as significant contributors to the creative and economic wellbeing of our communities.

As well as championing the art of writing for the stage by producing and presenting new plays, Live Theatre unlocks the potential of young people and finds and nurtures creative talent. It also leads and demonstrates future thinking on new models of business sustainability and growth.

Founded in 1973, the Theatre was transformed in 2007 with a capital redevelopment. The result is a beautifully restored and refurbished complex of five Grade II listed buildings with state-of-the-art facilities in a unique historical setting, including a 160-seat cabaret-style theatre, a studio theatre, renovated rehearsal rooms, a series of dedicated writers' rooms as well as a thriving café, bar and pub.

Live Theatre is a national leader in developing new strategies for increasing income and assets for the charity. In 2014 the company announced Live Works, a £10 million capital development to purchase and develop quayside-fronted land and buildings adjacent to the Theatre, to create a children and young people's writing centre, a public park and a new commercial office space.

Live Works will join the award-winning pub The Broad Chare, online course www.beaplaywright.com and The Schoolhouse (an office space for SMEs), as one of Live Theatre's creative enterprises, which increases funds through new income streams.

For more information see **www.live.org.uk**

Live Theatre's Education & Participation work

Live Theatre's award-winning Education & Participation team work and develop creative relationships with young people and local communities in the North East via three strands: Education, Youth Theatre and Community.

Education: Live Theatre leads exceptional theatre work in schools. The company's two flagship writing projects for primary and secondary schools *First Draft* and *Write Stuff* have resulted in many professionally produced performances at Live Theatre. In April 2013 *Michaela's Mistake*, a monologue written by 12 year old Chelsey Cleminson, was developed into a full production and toured to 15 schools reaching 1500 young people across the region. The piece, which tackles issues relating to social media grooming and child safety, was well received by students and teachers alike.

Live Theatre also delivers Theatre In Education projects, young writers projects, master classes for teachers, and drama and literacy workshops to support the curriculum.

In 2016, Live Theatre's work with young people will make a transformational change with the exciting new Children & Young People's Writing Centre as part of the Live Works development. The centre will be cutting edge, imaginative and will enable young people of all ages to use drama to unlock literacy by presenting stories in inspirational new ways.

Youth Theatre: Live's Youth Theatre is the largest free youth theatre provision in the North East. Every year nearly 200 young people aged 11 to 25 years old meet at Live Theatre, or at one of its satellite venues, to take part in drama sessions. The aim of the Youth Theatre is to tap into the creative potential of young people living across Tyneside and encourage them to use theatre and drama to develop key social and personal skills that will be of use throughout their lives.

Live Theatre offers guidance and support to young people who have an interest in pursuing a career in theatre and over the years has seen former Youth Theatre members working regionally and nationally as actors, drama facilitators, directors and administrators.

Community: Live Theatre is committed to delivering outreach work with young people in their communities. Workshops explore young people's thoughts, views, opinions and situations within the context of their neighbourhood.

In 2014 Live Theatre's Education & Participation team received regional recognition for its work by being awarded joint winners of Outstanding Contribution at the North East Youth Work Awards. In 2015 Live Theatre was awarded Investing in Children membership for its work involving children and young people.

To find out how Live Theatre's Education & Participation team can help your organisation please contact **education@live.org.uk**

Day of the Flymo

by Paddy Campbell

FOR AMATEUR PRODUCTION ENQUIRIES

UNITED KINGDOM AND WORLD EXCLUDING NORTH AMERICA

plays@SamuelFrench-London.co.uk

020 7255 4302/01

Each title is subject to availability from Samuel French,

depending upon country of performance.

Please note that text was correct at time of rehearsal and may differ from the live performance.

About the writer

Paddy is a Northern Irish writer based in Newcastle upon Tyne. In 2007 he completed Live Theatre's *Introduction to Playwriting* course and has worked extensively with Live Theatre since.

Paddy's work for the company includes the award-winning play *Wet House* which was named as one of The Guardian's Top 10 Plays of 2013 and toured to Hull Truck Theatre and Soho Theatre the following year. Other credits include: *Dial a Mate, The Potting Pelaw Python, I Just Feel So Special, Home Help, Angel 2106, The Group, Perjury* and *Tis The Season*. He has also had work produced in co-productions with National Theatre (*The Great Unwashed*) and Nabokov (*The Nest*). Paddy has also worked as a dramaturg on Live Theatre's young writer's projects, *First Draft* and *Write Stuff*.

His plays for other companies include *Flowerpet* (GIFT Festival), *One Small Case* and *My New Favourite Place* (Curious Monkey), *Breaking Point* (Northumbrian Touring Theatre), *The Conceptualist's Mam* (Ink Festival) and *School Run* (Sage Gateshead).

CHARACTERS

LIAM – 13.

BECCA – 16, Liam's sister.

KAREN – 30, Becca and Liam's mam.

BEN – Social worker.

CLARA – 15.

Note: A / denotes the suggested point of overlap between that actors line and the next.

Scene One

Living room. **BECCA** *sits on a sofa doing homework on her lap. She remains quiet and concentrated during the following.* **LIAM** *runs from stage right to left wearing pyjama bottoms and roaring.*

KAREN *(off)* Shit shit shit shit. Liam get – Look at the fucking time. Is Becca up? *(shouts)* Becca? Becca? Becca are you up?

BECCA *(unheard)* Yes.

KAREN *(off)* Liam get ready now. Now Liam, there's not time to– have you? Ah Liam shower quickly, I mean it.

LIAM I'm fine.

LIAM runs from stage left to right.

KAREN *(off)* You're not. Now Liam. Please.

KAREN enters wearing a dressing gown.

Becca why didn't you wake me?

BECCA I/ tried.

KAREN Give me your sheets Liam.

LIAM *(off)* He skips past the second defender, have you ever seen anything like this?

LIAM enters. He wears a t-shirt, boxer shorts and one sock. He is playing football with the other sock.

Could this be number six on his debut? He nutmegs Brown, now just the keeper to beat, I can't believe what I'm watching, listen to the crowd, he shoots, oh my god, oh my shitting god. What a goal! What a goal! Women's knickers are landing on the pitch and who can blame them? I might throw my knickers Alan. The entire stadium is going wild. The Gallowgate end's starting to collapse.

LIAM *pulls the front of his t-shirt over his head and runs round in circles celebrating and making the sound of a cheering crowd. He crashes into something and falls on his arse.*

AGH BASTARD!

KAREN *enters. She holds* **LIAM** *'s bedsheets in a bundle in one hand at arms length. She holds* **LIAM** *'s school trousers in the other, which she drops in front of him.*

KAREN Right, there's no time to shower. Will you get these on and go? For God's sake Liam.

Becca will you help?

BECCA *(without looking up from her work)* Nearly finished this.

KAREN *exits.*

KAREN *(off)* Bollocks!

Becca? Becca will you get washing powder on your way home?

BECCA *(unheard)* I'm going/ to Dad's.

KAREN *(off)* Liam you better be getting ready.

LIAM *resumes playing football with his sock.* **KAREN** *enters and screams at* **LIAM**.

NOW LIAM!

I swear to God.

Becca? Becca have you seen my purse? I'm sure I...

BECCA By the toaster.

KAREN exits. BECCA finishes her work, puts her books in her bag and stands to leave. KAREN enters with her purse.

KAREN Becca you'll have to go to the Scoop a Market and just get a couple of washes worth of powder.

BECCA I'm going round to Dad's after school.

KAREN You never said.

BECCA I've said about five times.

KAREN Oh.

Liam get your shoes.

LIAM exits passing close to BECCA.

BECCA Mam he can't go like that. He stinks.

LIAM *(off)* You stink.

BECCA You need to tell him mam.

LIAM enters with his trainers on.

KAREN Liam love, Becca's right. You'll need to get in the shower.

LIAM I've had one.

BECCA Has he shite.

LIAM Have.

KAREN Please Liam.

LIAM I'm fine.

BECCA You pissed the bed. You're not fine. You stink. Get a wash.

LIAM Fuck off Becca.

KAREN Liam!

Becca there's no need to be so…

BECCA I have to go mam. I can't be late.

KAREN Can you just wait ten minutes while he …?

LIAM I'm not getting in the shower.

BECCA I can't this morning.

KAREN Please love.

BECCA For God's sake.

> *The door is knocked loudly.* **BECCA** *stops.* **LIAM** *gets on his hands and knees and starts growling like a dog.* **KAREN** *freezes.*

KAREN *(whispering)* Shut up Liam, I mean it.

BECCA Mam?

KAREN Sssshhh!

> *More knocking.* **LIAM** *barks.* **KAREN** *kicks him.*

LIAM Agh!

BECCA *(whispering)* I have to go.

KAREN *(whispering)* No. Please.

BECCA *(under her breath)* Fucking hell.

> **KAREN** *motions to* **BECCA** *to crouch down so they can't be seen through the window.* **BECCA** *reluctantly complies. More knocking.*

BEN *(from the other side of the door)* Karen Karen, I can hear you in there. Look, you don't need worry. Just a quick chat to… you really have nothing to worry about. A quick chat to see if you might need some extra support with… we understand how difficult it can be. It's just Liam's attendance has fallen bellow…

LIAM Woof!

BEN Please. This is something we can easily work out.

Pause.

This would be so much easier if you'd just...

LIAM Woof!

Pause.

Please Karen.

Right I'm going to put a note through the door. Could you please ring me today so we can talk?

A piece of paper is pushed through the letter box. **LIAM** *crawls on his hands and knees and takes it in his mouth. He crawls back to* **KAREN***, drops it in front of her, pants like a dog and swings his backside from side to side like he's wagging his tail.* **KAREN** *puts her head in her hands.*

Scene Two

BEN Fifth of April, email received from Rob Martin *(Educational Welfare Officer)* expressing concerns about a recent dip in Liam's attendance. Rob has been unsuccessful in contacting Mum with a view to arranging a Personal Education Plan meeting.

Seventh of April, unannounced visit to family home. Liam failed to attend school that morning. No response, although voices could clearly be heard inside. Letter delivered requesting contact from Mum asap. As yet, no response.

Scene Three

Lane. There is a high garden wall and a wooden gate.
BECCA *is wearing a school uniform and calls for* **LIAM**.

BECCA Liam Liam, Liam for fu...

Liam come on.

Pause. A battered, half-flat football is thrown over the wall. **BECCA** *picks it up.*

Right come on Liam, we're gonna be...

What are you doing?

Pause.

BECCA *goes towards the gate.*

Liam?

LIAM *kicks the gate open breaking it. He runs on struggling to carry a Flymo lawnmower.*

LIAM YOU DICK!!

LIAM *trips on the chord and falls hard.*

LIAM AGGH! me knackers.

BECCA Put it back now.

LIAM *gets up.*

LIAM Run!

BECCA No.

BECCA *grabs one end of the Flymo and* **LIAM** *the other. They struggle against each other.*

Put it back.

LIAM No way.

BECCA Don't be stupid.

LIAM Could make a fortune with this.

BECCA Drop it.

> *A door is heard opening from the other side of the wall.*

Bollocks.

> **BECCA** *lets go of the Flymo.* **LIAM** *runs off with it.*

LIAM Come on.

BECCA Oh fucking hell.

> **BECCA** *runs after him.*

Scene Four

> **CLARA** *sits at a bus stop, she is listening to music on headphones from her phone.* **LIAM** *enters and sits next to her.*

LIAM Y'alreet?

> *No response.*

Y'alreet?

> *No response.*

Y'alreet?

> *No response.*

Bollocks man.

> **LIAM** *pokes* **CLARA**. **CLARA** *jumps, startled and takes her headphones out.*

CLARA Jesus! What?

LIAM Y'alreet?

CLARA Fine.

    CLARA *goes to put her headphones back in.*

LIAM What you up to?

CLARA What?

LIAM What you up to?

CLARA Well I'm at a bus stop.

LIAM People generally get on buses at bus stops.

CLARA Yeah well...

LIAM What you listening to?

CLARA I'm sorry would you mind –

LIAM I'm into loads of stuff me. Tupac, 50 Cent. Reckon people get better once they get shot. Do ye wanna buy some tack?

CLARA No thanks.

LIAM It's good gear, honest. Moroccan.

CLARA I'm fine.

LIAM Look.

    LIAM *shows her a brown lump wrapped in cling film.*

CLARA That's a bit of brown colouring pastel wrapped in cling film.

LIAM It's not like, good gear this.

CLARA No it is. It says Faber on it. I've got a set at home.

    Slight pause.

LIAM Sorry, I wasn't trying to jip ye.

CLARA Yes you were.

LIAM I was yeah. Sorry.

CLARA Look, I'm not really in the mood at the minute. Would you mind leaving me alone?

LIAM There's another bus coming. You getting it?

CLARA Yeah, I don't know. Look, sorry, please…

Pause. A bus drives past.

LIAM How come you're not at school?

CLARA Just not.

LIAM I've got bigger fish to fry me.

CLARA I'm sure you do.

LIAM Got meself a few sidelines. Gardening and that. School's a waste of time if you ask me.

CLARA I didn't.

LIAM Best getting yourself a trade. Ye na what I mean?

CLARA No offence, but you're like twelve.

LIAM I'm thirteen.

CLARA No one's going to employ you as a gardener. Have you even got any equipment?

LIAM Yeah loads. Well I've got a mower. This woman up Gosforth told us to come back at three to do her lawn. Reckon she's minted. Come with us if ye like.

CLARA No thanks.

LIAM Suit yourself.

CLARA Look, I'm gonna go.

LIAM Here's me card if you change your mind.

> LIAM *takes some Post-it notes out of his pocket. He has written his name and number on each one. He sticks one on* CLARA*'s arm. She removes it, reads it, sniggers and exits.*

Scene Five

BEN L was permanently excluded from Rosehill Manor School in February 2013. A series of incidents culminated in L making an improvised flame thrower with an aerosol and setting alight another pupils' school bag. Staff felt they were no longer able to keep L and his fellow pupils safe.

L has since been placed in Lonsdale Pupil Referral Unit. This transition has proved difficult for L and his attendance has been poor. L did initially work well with one to one tuition at the beginning of his time at Lonsdale. However, resources are not available for L to continue with one to one tuition and attempts to integrate him into classes have resulted in L disengaging from school completely. A Special Educational Needs report accompanies this document.

Scene Six

BECCA *and* **LIAM. LIAM** *is more hyper than usual.*

BECCA Will you not tell mam?

LIAM Why not?

BECCA Just.

LIAM Why though?

BECCA Cos it'll only make her… you know. I'd just rather you didn't. I'm gonna tell her it's a school trip that's part of the course. She doesn't need to know me dad paid. Please don't tell her.

LIAM All right.

BECCA And me dad hasn't told Beverly.

LIAM Has he not?

BECCA Reckons she'd go off it. Silly cow.

LIAM Why?

BECCA Think she kicks off when he gets me stuff and not them. She's a divvy.

LIAM Propa divvy.

BECCA Don't know what he's doing with her. Her fucking voice. Dad says vets pay her to spay dogs just by screeching at them.

LIAM *(laughs)* Does he?

BECCA Aye.

LIAM I bet he'll get you something mint if you pass your exams.

BECCA Dunno if I will.

LIAM You will. You're the cleverest person I know.

BECCA That's not saying much.

LIAM Piss off.

> **LIAM** *hits her a playful dig in the arm.*
>
> Could I come to your dad's next time your going round?

BECCA I dunno. Depends on her. I'll need to see.

LIAM He likes me though doesn't he?

BECCA Yeah he does, it's just her.

LIAM Will there still be dead bodies?

BECCA Where?

LIAM In the trenches you're going to.

BECCA Well not lying about. But there was thousands killed and blown up. So there's probably the odd head and foot underground.

LIAM *(laughs)* Do ye reckon?

BECCA Definitely.

LIAM Will ye have a dig for us? Bring us something back?

BECCA You're not gonna be allowed to start digging stuff up.

LIAM Aw go on, just a finger or something.

BECCA If I bring you a finger back will you go to school?

LIAM Yeah promise.

BECCA Have you been today?

LIAM I went for a bit in the morning. It was wank though.

BECCA Fuck's sake Liam Where have you been?

LIAM Check it out.

> **LIAM** *takes two ten pound notes from his pocket and waves them triumphantly.*

BECCA Where'd you get that?

LIAM Been grafting.

BECCA Jesus what have you done?

LIAM Honest, been doing gardening and stuff. Took the Flymo up the posh houses. First one I tried, this granny, her house smelt like a pet shop. I said a fiver to the cut lawn and she says aye so I do it, but the wire's not even long enough to reach the corners so I was gonna say three seventy five cos I couldn't reach it all but she said I'd done a great job then she says to come in for coffee and cake and I tried to say I couldn't drink coffee cos it makes me fucking nuts but she'd already done it before I got the chance cos she was just chattin on non stop granny chat.

BECCA Have you been drinking coffee?

LIAM Aye.

BECCA Jesus you can tell.

LIAM Can ye?

BECCA You look mental.

LIAM I feel off me tits. But then she goes right, wait'll ye hear this, then she goes, I swear down, she goes to us, right here's ten pounds for doing such a good job on the lawn. Now, how would you like to earn another ten pound?

Aye missus what you need doing like?

Come here. She goes, and we go over to the window. And she says, do you see that red car parked outside my house?

It was this well smart Audi.

She says, do you think you'd be able to put a lovely big scratch down the side of it for me?

BECCA No she didn't.

LIAM I swear down on mam's life.

BECCA Mam'd be dead about fifty times over the amount of times you've said that and followed it with complete bollocks.

LIAM It's true Becca, honest.

BECCA Did you do it?

LIAM Are you mad? Course I did it. I fucked a rock through the back window and all for good like, what d'ye call it …? Good customer service. Cos the lawn did look pretty shit to be fair.

BECCA You what!?

LIAM No cos I reckon right, when you're starting your own business you should like, do a bit extra then they'll get you to work for them again.

BECCA You're not starting your own business.

LIAM I just made twenty quid in under an hour. I'll only need to work two hours a day and I'll be laughing.

BECCA There's not gonna be an endless amount of radge grannies wanting you to smash cars up for them.

LIAM I can do other stuff, I'm not just a one trick pony.

BECCA You need to go to school.

LIAM It's pointless.

BECCA It's not pointless.

LIAM It's all right for you, you don't have to go to the spacker school.

BECCA It's not a spacker school.

LIAM You've got like predictions for GCSEs. All we do is play snap and make bird tables.

BECCA Well there's always gonna be birds needing tables.

LIAM Birds were doing fine before people started making them tables. Only a numpty'd waste his time making a table for a bird. He's going to us, need to make sure it's cut straight and sanded nice and smooth. As if the some robin's gonna fly past and say, How man, I'm not eating my dinner off that pile of shite, it's not been fucking sanded.

BECCA Well people buy them, and you're learning how to make stuff with your hands and that. You'll probably end up earning more than me.

LIAM Doubt it. Might see if that granny's looking for a bird table though.

BECCA Don't go back there.

LIAM No one saw us. I was like lightning, its fine.

BECCA You need to go to school. Ben's coming in a bit. He'll know you've not been.

LIAM Shite, I forgot.

BECCA And don't tell him about cutting grass, smashing cars, or nothing.

LIAM I won't.

BECCA Cos you know what you're like, when you get going.

LIAM I won't I'm not stupid. Everything's cush, that's all I'll tell him.

BECCA You had your pill?

LIAM Uh huh.

BECCA Liam?

LIAM I lost it.

BECCA You lost it?

LIAM Well I sold it for three tabs.

BECCA Jesus Liam.

LIAM Sticky Darren crushes them up and snorts them.

BECCA Coffee and no pill. Go and get one now.

LIAM Where's mam?

BECCA Bed.

LIAM Still?

BECCA I'm gonna get her up before Ben gets here. And don't tell him about that either.

LIAM What?

BECCA Mam in bed all the time.

LIAM I'm gonna fuck it up, I know I am.

BECCA You won't, just remember what we said. Do you wanna go through it again?

LIAM No I remember.

BECCA Every time you're about say something, stop and think. Is this gonna land us in the shit? And if it is don't say it.

LIAM Right.

BECCA I mean it Liam, it's important.

LIAM I won't say nowt.

BECCA And if he asks why you've not been going to school?

LIAM I know I know. I'll say I was getting bullied off this lad, but it's all sorted now and I'm not gonna miss any more.

They can't send us back there just cos I'm missing school?

BECCA Not just that is it?

LIAM What else?

BECCA Mam's not right is she.

Scene Seven

BEN L has a diagnosis of ADHD, completed by doctor Pollock in April 2007 when L was eight. He is prescribed thirty five milligrams of methylphenidate a day.

Further assessments have not been fully completed as L has refused to engage with professionals. Dr Pollock has indicated that behaviours displayed at school may be indicative of an Autistic spectrum or bi polar disorder. However, L's lack of engagement has meant that any assessments have been inconclusive.

Mum reports that incidents of L bed wetting have decreased since a prescription of oxybutynin was made in August 2013. However, isolated incidents do still occur. There have been reports of L smelling of urine

which has been another cause of L being victimised
and bullied by other pupils.

Scene Eight

Fast food restaurant. **BEN** *and* **LIAM** *sit at a table with*
food. **BEN** *is laughing.*

BEN Jesus Liam how could you tell it was...?

LIAM Felt a wind on my face. And it definitely came out
the front.

BEN Christ no!

LIAM And I wasn't rude or owt. Put my hand up, said
please.

BEN You said please!

LIAM I said, please miss could you not do fanny farts when
you're standing next to my face.

BEN can't help laughing.

BEN Liam man, you can't say stuff like that to teachers. Or
anyone.

LIAM She went fucking ape shit.

BEN I bet she did.

LIAM Then ran off crying the daft cow. I'd to go to the
deputy head, wasn't allowed to go go-karting. I hate
her, can't stand her.

BEN You need to try to think/ before –

LIAM I don't want some scruffy slut doing fanny farts in
my face. Specially when I'm trying to do questions
on *James and the Giant Peach.* Nay wonder I'm shite at
spelling.

BEN Still Liam.

LIAM Got her back though.

BEN Aw no. What did you do?

LIAM No, nothing.

BEN Liam?

LIAM Becca said not to say owt.

BEN Did she now?

LIAM It's nowt really.

BEN Tell us.

LIAM She'll probably never see it.

BEN See what?

LIAM You know in the library right, there's the record of births and marriages, and they'll let you look at it if you ask them. I went in and said I was doing my family tree and I found her, Mrs Yeats, her first name's Claire. I found her birth in the book and I tipexed out her dad's name and changed it, so for her dad it says, some bouncers.

BEN *(laughs)* Jesus man.

LIAM You're not gonna say?

BEN No. Liam, you're a nightmare.

LIAM I shouldn't have said. Becca said not to say owt bad.

BEN You don't need to worry about that.

LIAM Cos everything's cush now. You don't need to keep coming to see us.

BEN Do you not want me to? I thought we were having a good laugh.

LIAM We are. It's not that, just I'm gonna go back to school next week and stop the drinking and staying out all night, so you don't need to worry.

BEN Good man, I'd still like to see you though.

LIAM No need.

BEN Ah go on, it's a good laugh. Rest of my job's dead boring, just writing reports all the time.

LIAM What you gonna write about me?

BEN Well I want to put that you're going to school and not getting brought home by the police at all hours of the night. And that you're getting a wash. No offence, but you're lifting.

LIAM I'm not.

BEN You are like. Does your mum not chuck you in the bath?

LIAM Yeah loads.

Are you eating your chips?

BEN Go for it.

> **LIAM** *eats some of* **BEN** *'s chips.*

BEN So who is it you're knocking around with down Benwell?

LIAM Just mates.

BEN Mates are they? How'd you know them?

LIAM Just from about, ye na.

BEN Good mates are they?

LIAM Aye they're all right.

BEN I'm not so sure. They're older aren't they?

LIAM Aye, they're cush.

BEN You reckon?

> *Slight pause.*

I'm a bit worried about them you see.

LIAM They're sound.

BEN It always seems to be you getting caught for stuff. Never any of them.

LIAM That's not cos of them. And I'm stopping all that now.

BEN What I reckon is that they're putting you up to stuff, and cos they're older you're doing it to impress them.

LIAM It's not like that. I do what I want me.

BEN What about the night you ended up in hospital?

LIAM That was legal highs, you can buy them in a shop.

BEN That's not the point. It's the fact that they left you on your own rolling about in a car park in the middle of the night. If that woman hadn't've found you...

You see that's not really the sort of thing that good mates do, just leaving you there like that.

LIAM I was alreet.

BEN You weren't really Liam, you're only thirteen. Can you see why people are worried? Your poor mum must be worried sick.

LIAM Suppose. But I'm not going to do that any more.

BEN Good, and you're definitely not just telling me that cos you know it's what I want to hear?

LIAM No honest.

BEN How is your mum anyway?

LIAM Sound.

BEN Good.

LIAM Just doing like loads of normal mam stuff.

BEN Normal mum stuff? What like?

Slight pause.

LIAM You know, cleaning, not staying in bed, cooking buns and that, mam stuff.

BEN Cooking buns?

LIAM Aye cooking buns.

BEN What sort of buns does she cook?

LIAM Pink ones mainly.

BEN Pink buns. Nice.

You still getting on with Becca?

LIAM I love my big sister.

BEN Good lad. What does she say when you go missing at all hours of the night?

LIAM She gans off it.

BEN It must be worrying for her as well. Cos she really cares about you doesn't she?

LIAM Yeah I know.

BEN And she's got her GCSEs coming up. I'm sure she could do without worrying about you getting taken to hospital at all hours of the night.

LIAM Suppose. She's getting us to try and stop and think for five seconds before I do anything. Specially if the thing I'm going to do involves hammers or nicking stuff.

BEN Sounds like a good plan.

LIAM It's harder than you'd think.

BEN Well keep trying.

Slight pause.

LIAM Will I be allowed to keep living with me mam and Becca?

BEN Liam no one said anything about you not living with your mum.

LIAM Why else are you coming to see us?

BEN People are worried about you, that's all. You don't need to worry about not living with your mum.

LIAM It was proper shit the last time.

BEN I know, if you try your best to do these things then…

Slight pause.

Liam?

LIAM Yeah?

BEN How did you know, in the library, where to find your teacher's birth?

LIAM Looked at it before hadn't I.

BEN Had you?

LIAM Looked up my own.

BEN Why'd you do that?

LIAM Cos I know I'm not right, I could tell.

BEN Tell what?

LIAM I've got bad blood don't I?

BEN You don't have bad blood Liam No one's got bad blood.

LIAM I do, from him. Knew mam was lying.

BEN Liam, you haven't got bad blood, you shouldn't think that.

LIAM I do though. I used to believe her, after he went. She'd tell us he wasn't my real dad. My real dad was dead nice but got killed, and I was like him, not like that fucker. But it's all bollocks though isn't it?

BEN She was just trying... trying to protect you.

LIAM Everyone thinks I'm thick.

BEN You're not thick.

Pause.

Liam, just cos your dad did, well did some bad things, it doesn't mean that/ you –

LIAM I'm bad though aren't I?

BEN You're not bad. You get up to mischief. Maybe make some daft decisions. But you're not bad.

LIAM That's not what everyone else says.

BEN Well they're wrong.

Pause.

Liam listen, you haven't got bad blood.

LIAM The last time, before he got put away, the last time I saw him before he... I was just playing, mucking about with the kittens. The ginger cat Becca brought home that had the kittens. Can't remember the name of it now. Nancy. That was it. Nancy. And I was just messin about, and the kittens were feeding and I thought I'd – and it weren't like there was no milk in the fridge or nothing, but I just thought I'd try for a laugh.

BEN Try what?

LIAM Cat milk. So he came in and I was sucking the cat to see what the milk tasted like. I was lying on my tummy trying to suck the cat milk out of Nancy and I didn't know he'd come in. I didn't hear him. And he grabbed the back of my neck and pushed my head sideways on the floor and he grabbed Nancy in his other hand and he smashed it off the ground right next to my face.

Over and over and over again smashing her off the ground till her head was all broken and the wrong shape and she stopped making the noise. Then he made me go in the small room with him across the hall where there's the rubbish chute to the big bins. And he put the kittens down the chute one by one. Just shoved them down the chute. But the last one grabbed onto the side and pulled itself back up and scratched his arm. And it was running about the floor of this tiny little room and he jumped on it as hard as he could. It crunched and kind of burst. The blood went up my leg. He made me chuck that one down the chute and said if I was gonna behave like a fucking animal then I'd be going down there with them.

Slight pause.

I reckon I must have some bad blood in me.

BEN *can't speak and is struggling maintain composure.*
LIAM *eats some more of his chips.*

Scene Nine

Living room. **BECCA** *is sitting quietly doing homework.*
LIAM *tiptoes into the room.* **BECCA** *hears him but ignores him.* **LIAM** *has threaded a live bee onto a piece of thread. The bee is approaching death and hangs limply on the end of the thread but makes an occasional buzz. As* **LIAM** *approaches* **BECCA**, *starting quietly and getting louder, he sings the words, "bee on a string" to the theme tune of Dr Who. When he gets behind her he swings the bee at her face. She bats it away and shouts.*

BECCA FUCK OFF LIAM!!

What is that?

LIAM Bee on a string.

BECCA *jumps away scared, realising that it is actually a live bee on a string.*

BECCA You psycho! It could've stung my eye.

LIAM It's mint isn't it? I was hoping it'd still be able to fly with the string through it, but one of its wings came off when I was trying to get the needle through.

LIAM *holds the bee up, which now appears to be dead. He pokes it and it swings back and forth.*

Come on son.

BECCA It's dead Liam.

LIAM It were going a second ago. Hold on.

He pokes it again. Nothing.

Aye, think it is.

Pause.

Bit of an anti climax to be honest.

LIAM *drops the bee.*

BECCA What did you think was going happen if you stuck a needle through a bee?

How do you stick a needle through a bee anyway?

LIAM Thought it might be able to keep flying for a bit, but with the string through it like a lead. So what you'd have is like a miniature flying dog that could sting people, or, well... a bee on a string.

BECCA Liam you're mental.

LIAM It took fucking ages, you've gotta trap them under cling film against the window. And I tried just gluing the string on the first one, I'm not cruel, but the bee just got glued to the window. So this one got the needle. I held it down under cling film then you stick

the needle and thread through it, but it's hard not
to mash em when you're doing that bit. They're not
as squishy as you'd think, they kind of crunch. Think
I'm gonna give up on it to be honest and move onto
something else.

BECCA Shouldn't kill bees anyway.

LIAM They're twats man.

BECCA Bees aren't twats. World's gonna end when all the
bees are dead.

LIAM Divn't talk shite, who told you that?

BECCA Everyone knows it, Einstein said so.

LIAM Bees!?

BECCA They make stuff grow, spread pollen about and
that. When all the bees are dead we've had it.

LIAM I'm gonna do em all in. No no no I'm gonna do em
all in apart from the last two and I'd keep them in a
tab box. If you'd the last two bees in a tab box you
could pretty much rule the world. Everyone'd have to
do what you said or you could just destroy it all.

Pause.

I'd problees end up killing them anyway just to see
what'd happen.

BECCA Would ye?

LIAM You know what I'm like.

BECCA If you could end the world right now, just like that,
would you do it?

Slight pause.

LIAM It'd be too hard not to. Would'nt you?

BECCA No! Mam and everything, just gone.

LIAM But if it all happened at once no one'd really know, so like, if you think about it it'd be a nice thing to do.

BECCA Nice!?

LIAM Well we're all gonna die anyway. This way, no one'd be left behind missing people going boo hoo my baby's dead, it'd all just be everything gone in a second.

BECCA But there'd be nothing. Something's better than nothing.

Slight pause.

LIAM Suppose, there is that.

There is a buzz from the bee. **LIAM** *stamps on it.*

Scene Ten

BEN L was taken into local authority care on 21st October 2010 aged 9. L phoned an ambulance for his mum after she was assaulted by his dad. Mum was left unconscious with a shattered cheek bone and puncture wounds to her torso, which were inflicted with a broken bottle. L was instructed how to carry out first aid by a telephone operator while waiting for emergency services to arrive.

L was placed in Norton House Children's Home while mum recovered from her injuries in hospital. L's sister was staying with her dad, R, at the time of the assault and remained there while mum recovered.

Ls dad is due for release on the 25th of August. He is to have no contact with the family as part of his licence agreement.

Scene Eleven

Bus stop. **CLARA** *is sitting.* **LIAM** *enters.*

LIAM Alreet?

CLARA *(under her breath)* Oh Jesus.

LIAM Skiving again?

CLARA Not gardening today?

LIAM Nothing on today. Can you get served for tabs?

CLARA Never tried, but no.

LIAM Bet you would in Amir's. He serves anyone.

CLARA You go then.

LIAM I'm barred. He caught us stealing poppers. He'd definitely serve you. Please.

CLARA No. Where's Amir's anyway?

LIAM Up the West Road.

CLARA That's miles. I'm not going up there.

LIAM You're not doing owt else.

CLARA How'd you know?

LIAM You never do. I see you all the time.

CLARA What, you follow me?

LIAM I just see you hanging about, not doing owt. If you come up the West Road with us you can come round to Chantelle's.

CLARA Why would I want to go round to Chantelle's? Who's Chantelle?

LIAM Me pal. She just got her own flat cos she was in a care home and was meant to be moving back in with her mam. But then her mam launched a tin of spaghetti hoops off her neighbour's head and broke her eye socket and got sent down for it. So Chantelle got her own flat. It's a bit of a shit hole to be fair but she might have some drink in. Better than sitting about here.

CLARA Do you know what? I think I'll pass.

LIAM Suit yourself.

LIAM *sits. Pause.*

CLARA Aren't you going then?

LIAM Aye, in a bit. D'ye want rid of us like?

CLARA Just you said you were going, then you sat down.

LIAM I know, just Chantelle's more likely to let us in if I've got tabs.

CLARA She won't let you in unless you've got tabs? Doesn't sound like much of a friend.

LIAM She's alreet when you get to know her.

CLARA And when you've got tabs?

LIAM I'm not meant to go there any more cos I get into bother. But there's fuck all else to do.

CLARA You could go to school.

LIAM You can talk.

CLARA What about your business? You could do some gardens.

LIAM Hasn't really taken off. How come you're not in school?

CLARA Just. Can't face it today.

LIAM Yours is the stuck up one with just girls isn't it? Where you have to do the violin everyday.

CLARA You don't have to do the violin everyday.

LIAM That's not what I heard.

CLARA It is stuck up though. I hate it.

LIAM You've got to be minted to go don't ye?

CLARA Not always.

LIAM Are you minted?

CLARA No.

LIAM You sound minted.

CLARA No I don't.

LIAM You sound like that posh lezzer who presents the Olympics and the horse racing.

CLARA I do not.

LIAM Not in a bad way though.

CLARA Oh thanks.

LIAM Do they not phone up if you never go in?

CLARA Probably. My dad'll kill me. Literally kill me. All I get is how much it costs to send me there.

LIAM You've to pay to go to school!? Fuck that. They should be paying us to go.

CLARA I wouldn't go for a grand a day.

LIAM Can't be that bad.

CLARA It is, trust me.

LIAM Sure you don't wanna come up the West Road with us?

CLARA Positive.

Scene Twelve

Living room. **KAREN** *is asleep on the sofa.* **BECCA** *enters.*

BECCA Mam.

Slight pause.

Mam. Mam wake up.

BECCA *shakes* **KAREN**.

KAREN What! Jesus what is it?

BECCA Liam's still out.

KAREN What time is it?

BECCA Half two. Should we do something?

Pause.

Mam?

Mam we should do/ something?

KAREN What do you want me to do Becca?

BECCA At least get up.

KAREN Then what?

BECCA Don't you care?

KAREN I'm sick of it.

BECCA Don't say that.

KAREN I'm worn out.

BECCA From what?

KAREN Please Becca.

BECCA *(shakes* **KAREN***)* From what?

KAREN Becca don't.

BECCA *(shouts)* What's worn you out? You don't do anything.

KAREN Everything, Liam, I can't… I don't know if I can any more…

BECCA Why are you saying that?

Pause.

Mam, why are you saying that?

KAREN Living like this, it's like… it's like…

Sometimes I look at him and all I see is *him.*

BECCA That's not fair.

KAREN I know, but…

BECCA He's nothing like him.

KAREN Isn't he?

BECCA No, don't say that. He's thirteen.

Slight pause.

He used to try to stop it.

KAREN Rebecca please.

BECCA He did, he… after Nanna's funeral. You fell asleep. And Gary came in later in his suit, he'd a bleeding nose, fucking stank. And we could tell what was gonna happen. But Liam got up and lay on top of you, held on as tight as he could, to protect you. He did that.

KAREN I know he did.

BECCA You can't stop trying.

KAREN I am trying. Since I came out of hospital, all I wanted was to get both of you back and start over. Make things good for us…

Couldn't do it could I?

BECCA It's been good. Diggerland was good.

KAREN Come here.

They hug.

BECCA You can't just stop with him.

They separate.

KAREN Right. Right, ok.

KAREN *sits up.*

BECCA I've been ringing him, his phone's off.

KAREN Should we look? Go out?

BECCA You should report him missing.

KAREN Jesus, then they'll come round.

BECCA But how does it look if they find him and you haven't done anything?

KAREN The place is a state.

BECCA I've tidied. Ring them.

KAREN I'm sorry love, I'm shit.

BECCA You're not shit Mam.

KAREN I don't know what I'd do if... I'll sort it out, promise.

BECCA I know you will.

I'm going tomorrow morning.

KAREN Tomorrow!?

BECCA Had you forgot?

KAREN Sorry. Have you got everything you need?

BECCA Yeah, I'm packed.

I can stay if, if you need me/ to...

KAREN No no don't be silly. You don't need to worry about me. You have great time.

I'll miss you though.

BECCA I'll miss you to. It's only a week.

They hug.

BECCA You will, while I'm away…?

KAREN What?

BECCA Try, try not to let him… be firm with him.

KAREN Of course I will. Don't worry about that.

BECCA Just I know you've found it hard lately.

KAREN I know. I'm sorry. This new prescription, I've been a bit all over the place. But I'm getting used to it now. Honestly, you just have a good time.

BECCA Okay. You should call them.

KAREN Right.

They separate. **KAREN** *takes her phone and dials.*

Scene Thirteen

BEN L is becoming increasingly drawn to a negative peer group in the West End of Newcastle and mum states she is finding it more difficult to set any boundaries on L's behaviour. Incidents of L absconding and being returned home by the police under the influence have increased during the past month. An emergency care team meeting is to be held on the 4th of June.

Scene Fourteen

Living room, **KAREN** *and* **LIAM**. **LIAM** *is highly agitated.*

KAREN No.

LIAM Why?

KAREN I told you.

LIAM You've got it.

KAREN That's not the point.

LIAM I know for a fine fact you've got it.

KAREN I'm not gonna/ let you...

LIAM You got paid today. Four fucking pounds.

KAREN No. I know what you want it for.

LIAM I hate you.

KAREN Don't...

LIAM I do.

You can either give me it or...

KAREN What?

LIAM I'll rob someone.

KAREN Don't be fucking stupid Liam.

LIAM I will I'll do it.

> **LIAM** *exits. Sound of kitchen drawer being opened.*

KAREN Liam!

> **LIAM** *enters with a kitchen knife.*

LIAM Give me it or I'm/ gonna –

KAREN Put it down! Now Liam!

LIAM Just fucking give me it or I'm off.

KAREN No.

LIAM It'll be your fault.

> **LIAM** *goes to exit.*

KAREN I'm phoning the police the second you're out that door.

> **LIAM** *stops, turns and stares at* **KAREN** *for a moment.*

LIAM *(screaming)* JUST FUCKING GIVE ME IT YOU BITCH!

> **LIAM** *starts furiously stabbing the sofa while screaming. He is completely out of control.* **KAREN** *is terrified.*

KAREN Stop. Liam Stop.

> **LIAM** *continues to drive the knife into the sofa while speaking.*

LIAM She gets fucking anything she wants.

KAREN Who?

LIAM Becca.

KAREN What's Becca had/ that –

LIAM Her dad paid for France. I ask/ for –

KAREN No he didn't. The school paid.

LIAM He fucking did. Ask her. I get fuck all.

> *Slight pause.*

KAREN I didn't know.

Here, go, just go.

> **KAREN** *throws some coins towards the door.* **LIAM** *stops, he is hyperventilating.*

Go. There…

Go.

Leave the knife.

LIAM *drops the knife gathers the coins and exits.* **KAREN** *cries.*

Scene Fifteen

BEN Placement plan, Liam Saunders.

On the seventh of the fifth two thousand and fourteen a phone call received from mum stating L has threatened to take a knife from the family home and rob members of the public when his demands for money were not met. Mum states she is no longer able to cope with L and fears for his safety and the wider public.

L does not appear to have an awareness of the dangers he is putting himself in. He has stated that he is prepared to change his behaviour but has not displayed any actions to show this to be the case.

It is felt that at this point in time a residential placement away from the negative peer group he has been associating with would be best suited to L's needs. It is hoped that an initial three month residential placement, providing set boundaries and routines with structured family contact, will create stability for L and help him to re-engage with education. This will be followed by a structured re-integration to the family home.

Scene Sixteen

Living room. **BEN** *and* **KAREN**.

BEN This isn't a reflection on you.

KAREN *(laughs)* No not all.

BEN Anyone would need some support after...

KAREN It's like it's still happening, like he's still there, still...

BEN I know it must feel like that. But with Liam putting himself in these situations. I think we've reached a point where if something doesn't happen then...

KAREN I know. I know that. Still.

Slight pause.

BEN Right.

I'm going to need to go through this with you and get you to sign. Then maybe we could get some of his things gathered.

What time do you think he'll be back?

KAREN Not for a while yet.

BEN So we've a bit of time.

KAREN Yeah.

BEN *takes paperwork out of his bag.*

BEN Ok, this is a section twenty care order. Now, I don't want you to panic when you hear the words care order, because I actually think the wordings wrong. It's an agreement, not an order. There's no courts or anything like that. This something that we all agree to. And you'll still have full parental responsibility.

KAREN I don't see how I can have... ?

BEN Have what?

KAREN Responsibility. I don't see how I can have full parental responsibility when he'll be living in a children's home fifty miles away.

BEN Obviously the home will take over the day to day stuff.

KAREN What else is there apart from the day to day stuff?

BEN When we go over there the staff will explain everything. We'll sort out contact arrangements, make sure that's all in place.

KAREN How am I meant to get there?

BEN We'll make arrangements with the staff for visits. And as I explained, I've fought really hard for this, to get this placement for Liam Ofsted rate them really highly.

Slight pause.

KAREN Can I just ask?

BEN Yeah.

KAREN If I didn't agree to this? What then?

BEN Well… is that what you're saying? That you don't?

KAREN No I'm/ just…

BEN If you want me to go through the placement plan again or there's anything else that you're not sure about.

KAREN No I understand, I'm just wondering what would happen if I didn't agree?

Pause.

BEN Well… I mean obviously I'd have to go back to my manager and…

KAREN And what would he do?

BEN She, she would... I think with Liam's risks she would... I mean you've got substance abuse, offending, who he's associating with, his age, the hospital admission. I think it's probably likely, taking all of that into consideration, that we'd apply for a full care order, which would involve courts and... so that really wouldn't be in anyone's best interests.

Slight pause.

KAREN So I'm agreeing, but it doesn't really matter whether I agree or not cos its gonna/ happen anyway.

BEN Of course... of course it matters that you agree.

KAREN How?

BEN Because it means we have your support. That we're working together for Liam, and you'll support him through/ this...

KAREN Of course I'll support him.

Sorry, this is all just a bit... a bit...

BEN I know.

> **BEN** *puts a hand on* **KAREN**'s *shoulder. He puts the order and a pen in front of* **KAREN**.

You're sure you don't want me to go through anything again?

KAREN No.

> **BECCA** *enters with her bag having just returned from the school trip.*

Becca.

BECCA Hi Mam.

BEN Hi Becca.

Slight pause.

KAREN Did you have a good time?

BECCA What's happening?

KAREN While you were away, things got… with Liam, things got…

BECCA Got what? What's happened?

BEN Unfortunately, for Liam's best interests we've agreed/ that –

BECCA Mam what the fuck is going on?

BEN Becca. Over the past week, things have got much worse with Liam.

BECCA Worse how?

KAREN Becca, he had a knife. I thought he was… he was going to… there was nothing else I could do.

BECCA Thought he was going to what?

KAREN If you'd seen him. He was out of control. With a knife. I didn't no what else to do.

BECCA What did you do?

BEN We've agreed/ that –

BECCA What did you do?

BEN That for a period it would be best if Liam was placed some/where else.

BECCA No. Mam?

KAREN Becca I can't do it any more.

BECCA I fucking knew I/ shouldn't –

KAREN Please. Don't.

BECCA *(to* **BEN***)* She can't, but I can.

BEN Becca I know you think that. But it's just not viable for you/ to –

BECCA I can. It's what I've always done.

BEN I'm sorry. That's not an option.

BECCA Taking him away is though?

He listens to me.

BEN You're sixteen. We can't leave you with that responsibility. With your exams and...

BECCA Knew I shouldn't have gone.

KAREN He needs to get away from the divvys round here.

BECCA And who's gonna be living in this home with him?

KAREN Please Becca.

BECCA No seriously. It's not like you're sending him to boarding school.

BEN This is a good home. They've had great results with kids like –

BECCA At least he has us when he's here. Well me.

KAREN Don't.

BECCA He'll be by himself in a home full of fuck wits. He won't stand a chance.

BEN It's honestly not like that Becca.

BECCA I can't believe you're doing this to him.

KAREN Do you know what Becca? This isn't up to you. Okay?

Slight pause.

BECCA You're fucking useless. You really are.

BECCA *exits to her room slamming her door.*

KAREN Shit.

BEN Are you okay?

KAREN I don't know.

Is this the right thing?

BEN I think it is.

KAREN Okay.

BEN You're sure there's nothing you want me to go over.

KAREN No.

BEN Okay, if you could sign at the bottom there.

Pause. **BEN** *puts his hand on Karen's shoulder. She signs the order. Gets up and stands with her back to* **BEN**.

KAREN I've washed his stuff, I'll go and…

BEN Okay.

It'll be all right Karen.

KAREN It's the shame of it. When I had Becca that young, I was determined I wasn't going to fuck things up like everyone thought I would. And when her dad pissed off, even more so.

Then Gary came along. I didn't think anyone would be interested in us, with a kid at that age. I was pregnant with Liam when it started. It was shame. I felt ashamed. He made me feel ashamed. And after the last time when I was coming out of hospital and I knew he couldn't get to me any more. Becca was at her dad's and Liam was in care and yous where telling me to take time before they came back home. But no way, on top of what I already felt was I going to be the woman whose kids weren't allowed to live with her.

But it's happening now isn't it, so…

KAREN *exits.* **BEN** *puts the order in his bag.*

Pause.

LIAM *enters.*

BEN Hi Liam.

Scene Seventeen

Bus stop. **LIAM** *and* **CLARA**.

LIAM I'm a fugitive now you know. On the run. Been helicopters looking for us, sniffer dogs. It's fucking nuts. I can't tell you why I'm on the run though.

CLARA I didn't ask.

LIAM If you did though I couldn't tell you.

CLARA I'm not.

Pause.

LIAM Sometimes you've gotta take the law into your own hands though don't you.

CLARA I wouldn't know.

LIAM Say someone's punching your mam's head in. You're not just gonna stand there let em get away with it. D'ye na what I mean?

CLARA Not really.

LIAM D'ye want owt to eat? I've loads of propa nice scran.

CLARA No thanks.

LIAM Got meself quite a nice pad set up.

CLARA A nice pad? I'm sure you do.

LIAM It's the mother and baby changing room in the leisure centre. You can lock it from the outside with the pin off a fire extinguisher.

CLARA Sounds delightful.

LIAM No one ever checks it. It's out of order. Well it's out of order cos I bust the nappy changing table. No one's been to fix it all week. Don't think they're gonna bother. I go in just before they close for the night and you're sweet till the morning.

Slight pause.

CLARA What food have you got?

LIAM Finger food mainly. I've got twenty four mini smoked salmon bagels from Waitrose. The most of a macaroon selection pack. Sticky Asian chicken lollipops, which you're welcome to cos they're fuckin stinking. And seventeen bottles of Bulmers bold black cherry cider.

Come with us. It's gonna piss down.

Also there's a slow kid with a hearing aid sits outside Dixie Chicken most nights who'll definitely buy this lump of brown pastel off us for a tenner. I'm thinking of buying tabs with that and putting the rest away for a rainy day.

Scene Eighteen

BEN L talks openly about using alcohol, cannabis and legal highs. He states he has also tried ecstasy, speed and sniffed gas on one occasion. L states he does not feel his substance use is a problem. Appointments have been for L with drug and alcohol, services which he has not attended. L will not say where he receives the funds to pay for his use of substances. There has been police intelligence that at least one L's peer group has been involved in child sexual exploitation and there are serious concerns that L may be at risk of this.

Scene Nineteen

KAREN's *living room.* **BEN, KAREN** *and* **BECCA.**

KAREN Safer. You said he'd be safer.

BECCA Mam it's not Ben's fault.

BEN Look Karen –

KAREN He phoned, begging me to let him come home.

BECCA Mam getting pissed off isn't going to help.

KAREN Becca will you please just –

(*to* **BEN**) You promised me he'd be safer there.

BEN I know Karen, but you can't guarantee against/ every –

KAREN What happened exactly? They said attempted arson.

BEN Apparently he had a run in with another lad. One of the staff found Liam microwaving his glasses, I mean they had metal frames so it was quite dangerous. Anyway, when they tried to get him away from the microwave, that's when the bite happened.

I'm sure everything was done to try and keep him there and settle him in.

KAREN How? He bit someone and ran away and it doesn't sound like anyone did anything to stop him.

BEN That was the other thing. I'm afraid they're going to press charges about the bite.

KAREN Fucking fantastic.

BEN He broke the skin you see, so they needed a tetanus jab and tests. But the police said there's no evidence about the car/ so that's –

KAREN The car!? What car? No one mentioned a car.

BEN There was damage done to a car.

KAREN Fuck's sake.

BEN The manager Sylvia, when she went to drive home her exhaust had been tied to the drain cover under the car. The whole thing got ripped off. But there's no evidence that it actually was Liam. I mean it kind of points that way, but no proof, so at least that's something.

KAREN Oh well that's great then isn't it. No one knows where he is, he's wanted for assault, but at least they can't pin wrecking someone's car on him. I should try to get you in there and all Becca.

BEN I can appreciate how difficult this is Karen.

KAREN Difficult! Do not sit in my house and tell me you appreciate how fucking/ diff –

BECCA Mam!

KAREN Difficult.

BECCA Mam you need to calm down.

KAREN Shut up Becca!

Sorry, sorry I didn't mean to... I'm just...

BEN Look Karen, I'm sorry I really am. If Liam would just give them a chance. But they can't legally lock him in. But if he keeps doing this. Just disappearing and not working with anyone then...

KAREN What?

BEN Then we'll have to look at a secure placement.

BECCA Lock him up?

BEN Unfortunately. And if it were to come to that, it could be anywhere.

BECCA What do you mean anywhere?

BEN Where ever there's a place. It could be down south, Scotland.

KAREN Jesus no.

BEN It's the last thing I want to happen but there won't be any other option if…

KAREN Where is he?

BEN The police are doing everything –

KAREN Chantelle's. Have they tried there?

BEN They're making regular checks of all the people he's known to associate with.

KAREN They keep coming here. I keep telling them I'd let them know the second he turned up. But they keep coming anyway.

BEN I'm sure that's just a precaution.

KAREN Like I can't be trusted not to tell them.

BEN That's not the case Karen.

KAREN Doesn't feel that way.

BEN Karen, no one is judging you.

Slight pause.

KAREN Do you honestly believe the things you're telling me?

BEN The police have their own way/ of –

KAREN No, but when he was in the home? I'm sure the staff there did everything they could to keep him there.

Do you?

BEN Karen I'm trying to be as open and honest as I can.

KAREN Are you?

Slight pause.

BECCA Sorry Ben.

KAREN Don't you apologise for me Becca. You weren't here when he was telling me about this wonderful place they were going to put him.

BECCA No I wasn't here. First time I've been away for more than a weekend and look what happens.

KAREN starts to cry.

KAREN This was supposed to make things better. That's what you said.

BEN I hoped it would.

KAREN You hoped. That's great.

BEN There wasn't anything else I could've done. And I had to fight to get him in there and not a local authority home. I mean the cost is…

BECCA How much does it cost?

BEN No, I shouldn't have– the cost's not the point.

BECCA How much does it cost though, to send him there?

BEN I can't.

BECCA I can find out for myself.

Slight pause.

BEN They charge three grand.

KAREN Three grand a month!

BEN A week.

KAREN Three grand a fucking week!

BECCA What?!

KAREN Three grand a week!

BEN I know it's a lot but when you consider –

KAREN How can they pay that when– I can't replace his clothes and– Three grand a week!

BEN It's what they charge for an out of borough placement. And we pay them it.

KAREN If I'd an extra thirty quid a week, the difference that would make. What the fuck do they spend three grand a week on?

BEN Their costs. Paying the staff.

KAREN I can't believe this

Slight pause.

BEN It's what we do. The difficult kids we outsource to private companies and they make a profit. This shit situation you've ended up in, through no ones fault. And they make a profit out of it.

As long as something's being done. Even though that thing, time and time again, proves to be utterly useless. I put Liam in care because I had to do something and we'd tried everything else. I fought to get him in the best place we had. But still it's... sorry.

BECCA Just because this has happened, it doesn't mean there's no hope for him?

Slight pause.

BEN The first kid I got after I'd qualified. I see him all the time now, around Central Station.

He was twelve. His mum said she caught him, well, a sexual act on his younger brother. I mean not extreme... but still. And he always denied it. There was no evidence. But she was adamant, adamant she wouldn't have him in the house.

And you know. Even if what she'd said had happened. At that age, you don't necessarily know that what you're doing is... when your body's changing and you're mucking about. If you hadn't been told it was wrong then you wouldn't know. I honestly think it was entirely innocent if it even happened at all. But she wouldn't listen. And my manager said, if something were to happen in the future, and I'd put on pressure for him to stay at home, then that could look very bad.

So, care order. And there were several foster placements, none of them lasted long. His behaviour just went– I mean he was distraught, swore he hadn't done anything. And suddenly his entire world is completely dismantled.

We put him in a kids home, and school and everything went to shit. Drink, drugs, getting arrested. And he wasn't a bad kid.

But I see him now. All the time in town. He's nineteen and he's a mess. He'll be asking people for change, face all smashed in. He can't manage a flat, been kicked out of most of the hostels.

But the thing is, he's always so pleased to see me. It was me that typed up the reports that got him where he is. And he couldn't be happier to see me. Says I was someone who was always fair with him, decent.

Pause.

I don't know if I can do this any more.

BECCA You can't just give up. Because it's hard. What chance has Liam got if we all did that?

KAREN What can we do?

BEN When he turns up you've got to try to make him realise that this home is his only option now. If he keeps going missing then it'll have to be a secure placement.

KAREN I just want him home.

Scene Twenty

Mother and baby changing room. **LIAM** *and* **CLARA**.
CLARA *eats chicken lollipops and they both drink bottles
of Bulmers black cherry cider.*

LIAM I like the smell of swimming pools. I used to drink
the water.

Complete black out.

CLARA *(panicking)* Shit what's happening.

LIAM Oh yeah, they do that. I should have said.

CLARA Do what?

LIAM Turn the lights out for the night when they lock up.

CLARA Oh.

LIAM Are you scared?

CLARA It's a bit... a bit creepy.

LIAM You get used to it. When I'm on my own in here, it's
so dark it's the same with your eyes open or closed.
And there's the hum from the pool, you don't know
whether you're sleeping or awake. It's mint, it's like
you're floating. It's good that. I'm glad you're here
though, I'm not saying I'd rather be on me tod.

CLARA I'm glad you're here.

LIAM Honest?

CLARA Yeah.

LIAM That's good that.

> **LIAM** *attempts to kiss* **CLARA**. **CLARA** *pushes him away
> with all her strength.*

CLARA Get off us.

LIAM Sorry shit/ sorry sorry –

CLARA What the fuck are you doing?

LIAM Sorry I thought...

CLARA Thought what!?

LIAM I thought that –

CLARA I'm going.

LIAM No.

CLARA Where's the door?

LIAM No don't, please.

CLARA Where's the door?

LIAM No, you can't.

CLARA I'm not stopping here.

LIAM Please, there's alarms. They'll catch us if you open the door.

CLARA Shit.

LIAM I'm sorry, I just thought, shit shit, I'm a spacker. When you came with us I didn't think it was just for the scran and a drink, I thought maybes... most lasses take the piss out of us, even when they're not blatantly taking the piss out of us, I can tell underneath that they're still taking the piss out of us. And when you said you'd come back here with us I was fully expecting it to end up as some sort of piss take. But when it didn't I thought, ye na, I mean I'm thick, but I thought maybes she's interested in us in the romancing type of way, which is fucking stupid, I know. I mean, you're well pretty and not, well not a divvy and nearly sixteen, and I'm thirteen and living in a toilet. But then you came back with us, I don't understand, but then I never fucking do, that's nowt new. I've been thinking though, that it'd be proper mint if you were thinking along those lines, cos I'd treat you really well, you wouldn't need to worry about that. I know you could probably have any lad you like. I mean the lads I knock about with up in Scotchy, some of them were proper shit bags to lasses. Luke never took his chlamydia pills he'd get after the Hoppings and then he done Gemma just for the frisk of it. There'd be none of that, I promise. And well, I sometimes read me sister's magazines so I know what lasses are looking for... but you're not so... I'm going on, ignore us, I do that, I'll shut up now.

CLARA No don't.

LIAM Don't?

Slight pause.

CLARA I'm sorry you got the wrong idea. I'm just not really looking for a boyfriend at the minute.

LIAM Oh.

CLARA But don't stop talking. I like sitting in the dark listening.

LIAM Do ye?

CLARA Yeah I do.

LIAM How come you didn't go home?

Pause.

CLARA My dad he... I just couldn't go back tonight.

LIAM Why?

CLARA Is it all right if I don't go into that now?

LIAM Yeah.

CLARA Sorry just...

LIAM Will he be looking for you?

CLARA Probably, I've never done this before.

I'd like to just sit in the dark and listen to you talk. Is that okay?

LIAM Okay.

Pause.

Divint na what to say next.

CLARA Anything, doesn't matter.

LIAM Do ye wanna hear something me sister told us about bees?

Scene Twenty One

BEN L does not appear to have strong sense of his own identity and will behave in any way in which he feels will gain acceptance from those around him. He has found it difficult to maintain lasting and meaningful friendships and appears to have a low sense of self worth.

Scene Twenty Two

Mother and baby changing room. Morning, the lights have been switched on. **LIAM** *sits on the floor next to* **CLARA** *who is asleep and gently snoring. There are empty bottles of Bulmers black cherry cider.* **LIAM** *smells* **CLARA**'s *hair. The leisure centre* **TANNOY** *wakes* **CLARA** *with a jolt and* **LIAM** *jumps away from her. She cries out and sits up, at first unsure where she is. She is not aware of what* **LIAM** *was doing.*

TANNOY. AQUA/ AEROBICS WITH BABS IN FIFTEEN MINUTES, THAT'S AQUA AEROBICS WITH BABS IN FIFTEEN MINUTES.

LIAM I wasn't doing owt!

CLARA Jesus Christ!

LIAM Na it's just me.

CLARA What?

LIAM You snore.

CLARA Snore?

LIAM Aye.

CLARA I don't.

LIAM You do like. It was like trying to sleep next to a dog fight.

Sorry I had to take a shit. I was gonna flush it but I thought it might wake you up. I was a bit stuck with what to do for the best. Been sat here weighing up the options. Smell or noise, smell or noise. Smell's not so bad now. I put the lid down to stop it spreading.

CLARA Lovely.

LIAM What you up to today?

CLARA Is it morning?

LIAM I've to see a man about a dog.

CLARA What do you want a dog for?

LIAM Not actually a dog. But that's what you say isn't it.

CLARA Is it?

LIAM When you're up to something shady you say you're seeing a man about a dog.

CLARA Oh.

LIAM I'm not even up to owt shady, I just said it. I'm allergic to dogs. I've got me lawnmower stashed. There's this granny who's lawn I done. Reckon it'll have grown back by now. Gonna give her a knock. You can come with us if you like. Although she might want us to smash some cars up. That is a bit shady to be fair.

CLARA Do you just say things?

LIAM How'd ye mean?

CLARA Like the first thing that comes into your head. It's hard to keep up.

LIAM I swear down. She lives up by Hilda's World of Hats in Gosforth. Me mam says I'm always attracting nutters, divint na why.

CLARA But the other stuff?

LIAM What other stuff?

CLARA You haven't actually shot your dad with a crossbow?

LIAM Well I would've shot him with a crossbow but I was too small at the time and I didn't have a crossbow. But I will, when he gets out of jail I will, I'll be waiting for him. You watch.

> **LIAM** *demonstrates hiding and shooting his dad with a crossbow on his release from prison.*

Have that ye bastard.

CLARA I'll be honest, it's not the best plan I've ever heard.

LIAM I'm serious. One day I'll do him. You watch.

CLARA So how come you're …? if none of that happened.

LIAM Basically me mam can't cope with us cos I keep nicking off and getting off me tits and into bother. So me social worker put us in a home pure miles away in Consett. And they can kiss my hairy hole if they think I'm going back there.

CLARA That's shit.

LIAM Rights it's shit. I wanna try and say sorry and that to me mam and sister and let em know I'm alreet but without getting caught. Cos I was a fucking nightmare. Though I'm not right in the head you can problees tell.

CLARA You're all right you know.

LIAM I'm not like. I'm a tit.

CLARA No you're not.

LIAM I am, can't help it.

CLARA I bet you could. I mean you don't want to go for a sesh at Chantelle's now do you?

LIAM No but I'm chilling with you now.

CLARA Well you could just do this most of the time. I mean maybe not here but…

LIAM With you?

CLARA Yeah and with… there'd be loads of people would like hanging out with you.

LIAM There's not. People don't like us.

CLARA I like you.

LIAM Do ye?

CLARA Yeah.

LIAM Cheers. Yeah maybe. I wish it was like it was before.

CLARA When?

LIAM Before I done all that daft shite. Wish I could just go home and none of this was happening. Too late now. I've fucked it.

CLARA I'm sure you could sort things out if you put your mind to it.

LIAM Me social worker says if I'm good in the children's home then I can go home. But it's a shit hole. I never locked me bedroom door and I caught the kid in the room next to us cracking one off in front of a photo of me sister I'd stuck on my wall.

CLARA Ugggh!

LIAM Me mam probably doesn't want us back anyway.

CLARA I bet she does.

LIAM Doubt it.

CLARA I think, realistically, you might just have to stick it out at the home for a bit. If you want to get back to your mam's.

LIAM Yeah I do.

CLARA And you should keep your door locked while your there.

LIAM What about you?

CLARA What about me?

LIAM You never said why you're not going home.

CLARA No I didn't. My dad's a dick as well.

LIAM Does he hit you? Cos –

CLARA No, not that, but…

LIAM What?

CLARA It's hard to explain.

LIAM Right.

I'll sort him out for you if you want. I will honest.

CLARA No you're all right.

LIAM I've figured out the perfect murder. Completely untraceable. Need to get hold of an angle grinder for the teeth.

CLARA I don't want him… I just don't know what'll happen when I go back. He, well he locks me in. He pays all this money for my school and he doesn't think I try. I do, I just can't take anything in. And he accuses me of seeing boys and lying about where I've been. He stabbed my phone.

LIAM He what?

CLARA He called me downstairs and he had my phone on a chopping board and he stuck a big knife through the middle of it.

LIAM He sounds like a fucking psycho.

CLARA I think there's something wrong with him. But it's impossible to speak to him or…

I mean he'll apologise but then, sometimes like ten minutes later he starts accusing me of something else, or trying to trick him.

It's been getting worse. A woman who used to work for him is taking him to court. That's coming up soon and I think his business and everything could go if he loses. I honestly don't know what he's going to do next.

LIAM I mean I know you're nearly sixteen and all but I'll look out for ye. Anything you need sorting just say the word.

CLARA *is touched.*

CLARA I don't know what I'm going to do.

LIAM *puts his arm around her.*

LIAM Hey it's alreet pet. We'll be cush here.

CLARA What are you gonna do? Actually?

LIAM Howd ye mean?

CLARA You can't stay here forever.

LIAM I'll think of something. I reckon the pair of us'll alreet. If we stick together.

CLARA I'm going to have to go home and face it?

LIAM Are ye?

CLARA Yeah.

LIAM Are ye scared?

CLARA Yeah I'm scared.

LIAM Stay with me. I'll look after you.

CLARA Thanks. The longer I'm away the worse it's gonna be though.

LIAM You should tell someone.

CLARA I dunno, maybe I'm just being stupid.

LIAM I reckon you should.

CLARA There's nothing to tell really.

LIAM Doesn't sound like it.

CLARA It's not that easy though.

LIAM Me social worker Ben would know what to do.

CLARA I don't want to end up in some home.

LIAM Probably wouldn't come to that. Ben sent me mam on a parenting class. He'd probably send your dad on it.

CLARA He'd go ballistic.

LIAM I think you should talk to him before you go home. I'll give you his number.

CLARA Yeah maybe.

> *There is loud banging at the door.* **LIAM** *and* **CLARA** *get to there feet.*

VOICE. RIGHT OPEN UP IN THERE!

LIAM *(whispering)* Shite.

VOICE. OPEN UP OR IT'S THE POLICE.

> **LIAM** *goes to the door.*

LIAM *(whispering)* Leg it on three. Ready?

> **CLARA** *looks terrified.* **LIAM** *counts down from three with is fingers. There is more banging on the door.*

VOICE. FINE IF THAT'S HOW YOU/ WANT –

> **LIAM** *quickly turns the lock and shoves the door hitting the person at the other side.*

VOICE. AGH! BASTARD/ GET BACK HERE!

LIAM RUN!

> **LIAM** *runs for it.* **CLARA** *hesitates then follows.*

Scene Twenty Three

> **KAREN**'s *living room.* **KAREN**, **BECCA** *and* **LIAM** *enters, he looks terrible, dirty and wet.*

KAREN Liam! Liam oh god.

> **KAREN** *gets up, clings to him.*

Jesus Liam…

LIAM I'm sorry mam.

KAREN No no. I'm sorry. Come here.

She holds him tighter. **BECCA** *joins the embrace.*

BECCA Aw man you stink.

LIAM You stink.

KAREN You are lifting. Here take this off.

KAREN *removes his top, takes him to the sofa and wraps a blanket around him.*

Where have you been?

LIAM Don't make me go back there.

KAREN *breaks down.*

Please mam. I'll be good. I swear mam, I'll be good.

KAREN You are good. You are good Liam.

LIAM Don't make me go back.

KAREN Liam.

LIAM I promise mam. I'll do anything you want. Please mam.

KAREN Liam I…

LIAM I love you. I'm sorry.

KAREN *is distraught. She clings to him.* **LIAM** *cries.*

Please don't make me.

KAREN I can't Liam.

LIAM Why? Just let me stay.

KAREN I want you to. I want you to so much. It's not/ that –

LIAM Then do. Please mam.

BECCA We have to call them.

LIAM Don't.

KAREN Becca's right.

BECCA The police keep coming round. If they find you here and we haven't told them we're knackered.

LIAM I'll hide.

KAREN We can't Liam.

LIAM Please. If you phone them I'm off.

KAREN Listen, they're gonna lock you up if you keep doing this.

LIAM They won't find us.

BECCA Don't be stupid Liam.

KAREN Ben said if you went back and did what they asked you, stopped running away all the time then they could see about you coming back home. If you do it for three months/ then –

LIAM Three months is ages.

KAREN I know but –

LIAM It's shit. I hate it.

KAREN You didn't give it a chance.

BECCA He did say that Liam, honest. You've got to stop doing this though.

LIAM Don't. Wait please.

My lass is outside. I promised we could help her.

BECCA What?

LIAM She is. Honest.

KAREN Who's this?

LIAM She's not a knacker. She can play the clarinet. I said we could help her.

BECCA Help her with what?

LIAM She's got no where to go.

KAREN Jesus Liam, this is bad enough/ without –

BECCA Who is she?

LIAM Clara, she's called Clara. She's nice.

KAREN I'm sure she is just –

Right go and get her. Quickly, it's pissing down.

LIAM Reet. She's sort of my lass but don't mention it yet. It's early days.

LIAM *exits.*

BECCA Mam we can't have Christ knows who landing on the doorstep.

KAREN I know but... we need to keep him here. He's likely to do a runner if we send her packing.

BECCA Tell her she can get a warm then she'll have to go home.

KAREN Okay. I will.

LIAM *enters followed by a sheepish* **CLARA.** **CLARA** *is not what* **KAREN** *and* **BECCA** *were expecting.*

LIAM This is me mam and me sister Becca.

CLARA Hello.

KAREN Hello love.

BECCA Hiya.

KAREN Where have yous two been then?

LIAM Been camping out in the leisure centre. It was quite nice actually/ we –

BECCA Hold on.

LIAM What?

BECCA Has?

Sorry what's your name?

CLARA Clara.

BECCA Have you not been home?

LIAM She can't.

KAREN Christ sake.

LIAM Her dad's a proper psycho. He locks her up.

CLARA (*to* **LIAM**) Don't say…

KAREN (*to* **CLARA**) When did you last go home?

CLARA …

KAREN When did you last go home pet? Are you missing. Are people looking for you?

CLARA I don't know.

BECCA Mam we should ring Ben.

CLARA Sorry I… I'll go.

> **CLARA** *goes to exit.*

LIAM Wait. No let her stay for a bit.

> **CLARA** *stops.*

You can't just boot her out. It was her persuaded us to come back in the first place.

KAREN (*to* **CLARA**) Thank you.

BECCA She can't stay now though. Things are bad enough without us having another missing person here as well.

LIAM She's my best pal and you're kicking her out.

BECCA You only just met her. We're trying to help you.

CLARA I'll go.

LIAM No don't.

CLARA I'll be all right.

LIAM You don't understand. Her dad's a nutter.

KAREN *(to* **CLARA***)* Where do you live?

CLARA ...

KAREN Where do you live pet?

LIAM *(to* **CLARA***)* Ben could help you.

BECCA We need to phone Ben now.

> *Without warning* **CLARA** *runs out the door.*

LIAM NO!

> **LIAM** *goes to run after her.* **KAREN** *grabs him. They struggle.*

KAREN LIAM! LIAM /STOP!

BECCA DON'T LIAM!

> **LIAM** *breaks free of* **KAREN**. *He gets to the threshold of the door.*

LIAM I'm not gonna just leave her. She's got no one else.

KAREN Please Liam. Don't. LIAM STOP!

> **LIAM** *stops in the doorway.*

BECCA They'll lock you up Liam.

KAREN Please Liam.

Scene Twenty Four

BEN Staff report that after initial difficulties L has now settled in well to the home. He enjoys good relations with the staff team and most of his peers. L is responding positively to an incentive programme, which has been put in place to encourage him to attend education.

C made a self referral to social services having gone missing from home. An initial care team meeting was held at her school. Dad acknowledged that pressures at work in recent months had caused him to react disproportionately with C. It was agreed that C can stay with a paternal aunt to provide respite for Dad and a family support worker has been assigned.

Scene Twenty Five

Living room. **KAREN**, **LIAM**, **BECCA** *and* **CLARA** *They are celebrating* **BECCA**'s *GCSE results. There are Christmas crackers, a cake and a wonky bird table.* **KAREN**, **LIAM** *and* **CLARA** *wear paper hats.* **KAREN** *holds out a Christmas cracker to* **BECCA**.

BECCA It's not even Christmas.

LIAM So.

KAREN Ten As in GCSEs is better than Christmas.

LIAM Ten As and a C.

BECCA *sighs and pulls the cracker. It doesn't go off.*

LIAM Gimme the banger. Gimme the banger.

LIAM *pulls out the banger part and bangs it.*

KAREN Put your hat on.

BECCA Aw mam.

KAREN Go on.

BECCA It's pink. I'll look like a dick.

KAREN We all look like dicks.

>**BECCA** *puts the hat on.*

LIAM You do look like a dick like.

>**LIAM** *takes the joke from the cracker.*

>*(to* **CLARA***)* You do this one.

>**LIAM** *gives the joke from the cracker to* **CLARA**.

CLARA Do I have to?

LIAM Yep.

CLARA *(reading from the joke)* What's white and goes up.

LIAM Cocaine.

KAREN Liam! For Christ's sake.

CLARA A confused snowflake.

BECCA That's terrible.

LIAM It's definitely cake time now. I'm cutting it, I'm cutting it.

KAREN All right. Be careful.

>**LIAM** *exits to the kitchen and returns with the biggest knife he could find.*

BECCA Jesus Liam.

KAREN That's too big.

LIAM It's cush.

>**LIAM** *starts to haphazardly cut the cake.*

KAREN Do Ben a slice.

LIAM I divn't want him to take us back there.

KAREN Just another week love. If you're good.

LIAM I have been good. Look at that bad boy. That's worth at least four GCSEs right there.

He gestures proudly to his bird table.

KAREN I know. I'm proud of you.

I'm so proud of the both of you.

KAREN *momentarily appears overcome with emotion.*

BECCA Jesus mam, pull yourself together.

KAREN I am though.

There's a knock at the door.

LIAM If that's Ben already I'm not going back yet. He can piss right off.

KAREN Less of that.

LIAM I'm not though.

KAREN *exits.*

Tell him I'm going yet.

Door is heard opening (off).

KAREN *(off)* No no no. You can't… you can't…

GARY *(off)* Wait. Please, listen.

LIAM Mam!

GARY *(off)* Just let me see my boy. That's all I'm here for.

LIAM Fucker.

LIAM *runs off with the knife before anyone can react.*

GARY *(off)* There he is. Hey I got you –

KAREN *screams.*

Scene Twenty Six

BEN On the fourteenth of August two thousand and fifteen Liam's dad, G, was released form HMP Durham and immediately breached his licence conditions by returning to the family home. L, fearing his mum would be attacked, inflicted a stab wound on G. G sustained a ruptured spleen causing severe internal bleeding and resulted in a splenectomy. A grade five injury was also sustained to the left kidney, which was shattered along with tearing to the left renal artery.

L has pleaded guilty to Section 20 Grievous Bodily Harm against his Dad and is being held in Woodburn Young Offenders Institution to await sentencing. A full psychological assessment of L is to be carried out before he is sentenced to determine the degree of culpability, which can be attributed to L.

Scene Twenty Seven

LIAM, BEN *and* **KAREN** *stand outside the front of the court building.* **LIAM** *is smartly dressed and is uncomfortable in these clothes, tugging at them constantly.* **KAREN** *smokes an electronic cigarette.*

BEN It doesn't matter mate.

LIAM No one else's has a pink tie. I'm fucked.

KAREN You're not. It doesn't make any difference.

LIAM All the other solicitors are in like proper dark blue or navy. Mine comes prancing in like he's on *Strictly Come Dancing.*

BEN Hey, I've got a pink tie.

LIAM Well you would.

KAREN Liam!

BEN Why don't we focus on what he said, instead of the colour of his tie? Cos that all sounded really hopeful.

LIAM I should leg it while I've got the chance.

KAREN Don't be stupid Liam.

BEN Listen mate, let's go through it once more.

LIAM Do I have to?

BEN Please, it's important.

LIAM What's a spleen anyway?

BEN It's an organ that makes blood cells to help you fight infections.

LIAM And they took his out cos I knacked it. So he might die of something else later on. Get in.

KAREN Stop Liam! For Christ's sake.

LIAM What?

BEN Seriously mate. You can't say stuff like that.

LIAM It's true.

BEN Well keep it to yourself for today. Just stick to do what the solicitor said. Okay?

LIAM Right.

BEN Okay so, you saw him there shouting at your mum. And you thought –

LIAM I know I know, I thought he was going to hurt her. And I just did it without thinking.

BEN Good. Nothing else about wishing you'd finished him off. Or hunting him down. Got it?

Slight pause.

Liam?

LIAM Aye, I've got it.

BEN Good lad.

LIAM I bet he still sends us down.

BEN The solicitor doesn't seem to think so. Reckoned this is the best judge you could've hoped for. And if anyone knows it'd be him, whether he's in a pink tie or not.

LIAM Suppose. I've just got a feeling though. I'm the type of person gets locked up.

KAREN No you're not.

LIAM I am though. Everyone else in there was radge like me.

BEN You're not radge.

LIAM I stuck a massive knife in my dad. And we're saying it's cos I thought he was gonna hurt you mam. But I wanted to do it anyway.

I used to think about it all the time. Always imagined a big fight and, I'd have done loads of weights first and skipping, so I'd be strong enough. But it was easy, it was like…

Remember when I was a kid, I used to go mad for putting things in post boxes. I couldn't go past one without having to post something in. You used to lift us up. Just stones or crisp packets, anything that was lying about I'd stick in the slot. And it was like that, when I stuck the knife in him. It was just like putting something in a post box. Easy.

Slight pause.

I'm exactly the type of person gets locked up.

KAREN You were trying to be good.

LIAM I dunno.

BEN It's gonna be all right Liam.

LIAM I'm going for a piss.

KAREN Again! That's about twelve times in the last hour.

BEN We'll see you in there. We should head back up.

LIAM Right.

> **LIAM** *goes to exit.* **KAREN** *puts the electronic cigarette in her bag.*

BEN Wait. Hold on.

LIAM What?

BEN Almost forgot. It's Clara's birthday tomorrow. I'll take you round to see her if…

LIAM She probably won't want me there.

BEN No she asked me.

LIAM Did she?

BEN Yeah, about six times actually. And a text. Look.

KAREN Hey that'll be good.

> **BEN** *shows* **LIAM** *a text which he is elated by.*

BEN Thought we could go out and buy her something first.

LIAM Mint.

BEN Providing things work today obviously.

LIAM They might mightn't they?

BEN Yeah they might.

> **LIAM** *exits.*

> *(to* **LIAM***)* We'll see you in there.

Karen?

KAREN Yeah.

BEN How are you?

KAREN I'm… you know, I'm scared.

I just hope he comes home today.

BEN Me too.

And you think… if he does. Do you think you'll be able to manage?

Pause.

Karen?

KAREN What will this have done to him?

BEN *puts a hand on* **KAREN** *'s shoulder.*

BEN I'll help. I promise, I'll do everything I can to help.

KAREN I need to do it though. Not you or Becca or…

I need to do this.

BEN You can.

We should go in.

KAREN Yeah.

They exit.

Fade to black.

The end.

Property Plot

Costume:

Liam: Pyjama bottoms (p1), T-shirt, boxer shorts, one sock (p1), smartly dressed (p71)

Karen: Dressing gown (p1)

Becca: School uniform (p6)

Homework (p1)

Bedsheets in a bundle (p2)

School trousers (p2)

Puts her books in her bag (p3)

Purse (p3)

Trainers (p3)

Piece of paper (p5)

High-walled garden (p6)

Wooden gate (p6)

A battered, half-flat football is thrown over the wall (p6)

Flymo lawnmower (p6)

Bus stop (p7)

Listening to music on headphones from her phone (p7)

Brown lump wrapped in cling film (p8)

Post-it notes (p9)

Two ten pound notes (p12)

Fast food restaurant - a table with food (p17)

Chips (p19)

Homework (p24)

Threaded a bee onto a piece of thread (p24)

Sofa (p31)

Karen's mobile phone (p34)

Kitchen knife (p35)

Throws some coins towards the door (p36)

Takes paperwork out of his bag (p38)

A pen (p40)

Becca's bag (p40)

Pen (p43)

Ben's bag (p43)

Sticky Asian chicken lollipops (p52)
Bottles of Bulmers black cherry cider (p52)
Mother and baby changing room (p52 & p56)
Empty bottles of Bulmers black cherry cider (p56)
Wraps a blanket around him (p63)
Christmas crackers (p68)
A cake (p68)
A wonky bird table (p68)
Paper hats (p68)
Takes a joke from the cracker (p69)
Biggest knife he could find (p69)
Electronic cigarette (p71)
Karen's bag (p74)
Ben's mobile phone – shows Liam a text (p74)

Lighting Plot
Complete blackout (p52)
Morning, the lights have been switched on (p56)

Sound Effects Plot
The door is knocked loudly (p4)
More knocking (p4)
More knocking (p4)
Door heard opening (p7)
Ben speaking from the other side of the door (p4)
A bus drives past (p10)
Buzz from bee (p27)
Sound of a kitchen drawer being opened (p35)
Becca slamming her door (p42)
The leisure centre tannoy wakes Clara with a jolt (p56)
There is a loud bang on the door (p62)
More banging at the door (p62)
There's a knock at the door (p70)
Door heard opening (p70)

Group Discussion Points

Liam

- Does Liam really have 'bad blood' or is he a victim of his circumstances?

- Should Liam be able to stay at home?

- Has the care system failed Liam?

- What does Liam want from Clara?

- Is there any hope for Liam? Can he turn things around if he gets a favourable judgment at the end of the piece?

Becca

- What is Becca's role within the family?

- What is Becca's relationship like with her mother?

- What are Becca's coping strategies?

- How does Becca protect Liam?

- What factors helped Becca to achieve good GCSE results against all the odds?

Karen

- Is Karen a bad mother?

- Why is Karen struggling to cope with Liam?

- Does Karen need support?

- What kind of relationship does Karen have with Liam and Becca?

- Will Karen be able to cope with Liam if he gets a favourable outcome in court?

Clara

- Did Clara need to run away?

- How do Clara's experiences differ from Liam's? Are there any similarities?

- Why did Clara become friends with Liam?

- Why did Clara find it difficult to open up about her experiences with her Dad?

Ben and the care system

- At what point should the state get involved in the care of young people?

- Was Ben right in recommending a residential placement for Liam?

- Is there a lot of pressure on social workers in relation to the care of children and young people?

- What changes should be made in the way that the state deals with children and young people in care?

Character Exercises

Materials needed: paper, pens and crayons.

Character Bedrooms

Ask each actor to find a space in the room. They have ten minutes to imagine, in as much detail as they can, their character's bedroom. This will include the furniture, the colour of the walls, pattern of the bedspread etc. If they have a stereo what music is on it? Do they have a computer, laptop, tablet, smart phone, TV? What films do they watch? Where do they keep their clothes? What clothes do they have? Is the room tidy or messy?

After the ten minutes preparation time the actors will take it in turns to give the rest of the cast a tour of their bedroom, describing it in as much detail as they can and in response to questions from the rest of the group.

Character Senses

If your character was a... Taste, Smell, Sound... what would they be?

What would they be if they were: An animal? A flower? A musical instrument? A piece of music?

Discuss these as a group.

The actors are then asked to draw the shape, colour and texture of the character they are playing. The director asks the actors about the choices they made and why. This exercise is particularly useful when working with young people but works equally well with experienced professionals.

Role on the Wall

Each actor draws the shape of their character on a large piece of paper. (This can also be done drawing round each actor on a roll of paper.) Assign a different colour to each character.

Each actor or group finds a space in the room. In the head of the character outline, the actor writes how their character thinks and how they see themselves. In the body, they write how their character feels. They can use quotes from the text to support these opinions if they feel it is needed. Around the outside of the outline, write how they think other characters see them.

Leave the papers in their place and ask the actors or groups to move around each character outline. Using the colour that represents the character they started with, each actor or group writes what they think their character thinks of each of the others. This again can be supported by quotes if needed. A group discussion follows.

Hot Seating

This is a well used technique in rehearsal rooms. Each character takes the hot seat and is asked a whole range of questions from other members of the cast. This exercise always throws up questions that are not addressed by the text and is particularly useful for adding more flesh to the bones of the character during the early stages of rehearsal.